IRMA E. WEBBER

UP ABOVE AND

DOWN BELOW

YOUNG SCOTT BOOKS

Originally printed in 1943
All Rights Reserved
A Young Scott Book
Addison-Wesley Publishing Company, Inc.
Reading, Massachusetts 01867
Library of Congress Catalog Card No. 43-51044
ISBN: 0-201-09383-9
Printed in the United States of America
CDEFGHIJKL-WZ-89876543210

Ever so many kinds of animals live above
the ground.

Some animals live below the surface of the
earth.

Some of the animals spend part of the time above the ground

and part of the time in holes in the ground.

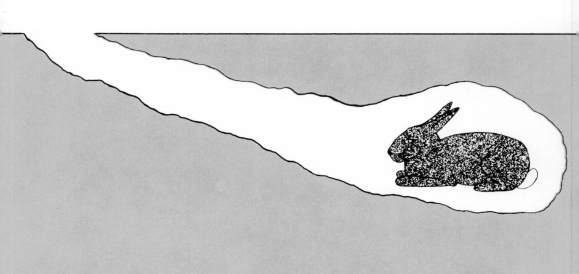

But a green plant grows with part of its body above ground

and part of its body below ground.

Sometimes the part above ground is tall and thin, like a poplar tree

while the part below ground may be made of roots that spread way out without growing down very far.

Sometimes it is the part above the ground that spreads way out, like a big shady oak tree

and the part below has a tap-root that grows down and down without branching much.

Sometimes the part that is up above is made mostly of leaves

and the part below is a fat root, like a carrot.

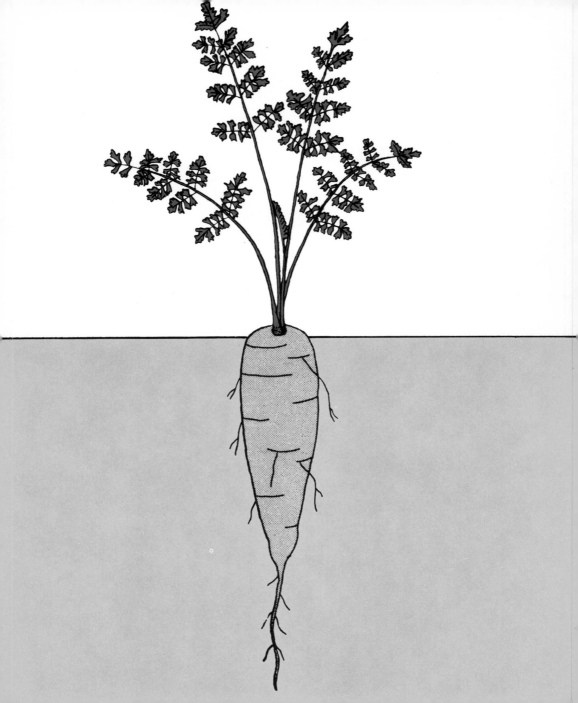

Corn has a tall stalk up above

and a bunch of little roots down below.

This is what an onion looks like above ground.

The part that we eat is the bulb under ground.

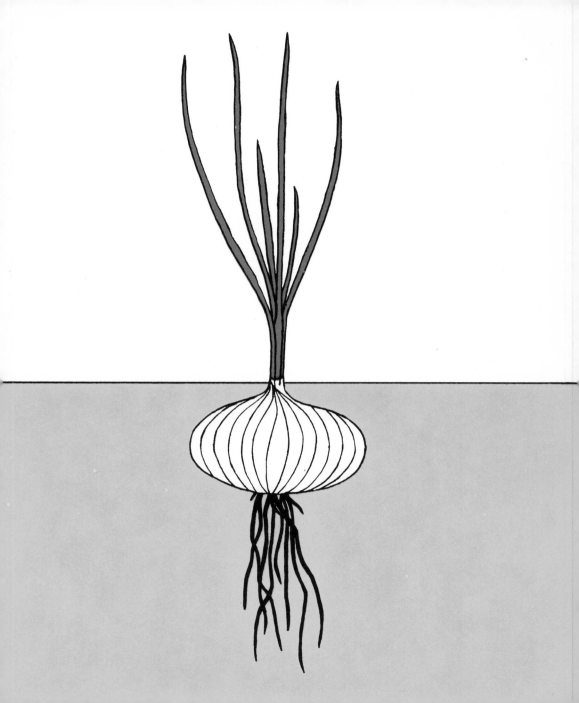

Up above there may be green stems and leaves

and below, a cluster of roots and swollen stems called tubers, or potatoes.

Whatever a plant looks like, the part above ground has air all around it

and the part below has earth all around it.

When the sun shines there is light as well as air around things above ground.

If we could see under ground with a magnifying glass, we would find that earth is made of tiny bits of minerals and humus, with air and water in the spaces between.

When there is sunlight above ground, green plants make food from the air they take into their leaves

and from the mineral-filled water their roots take from the earth.

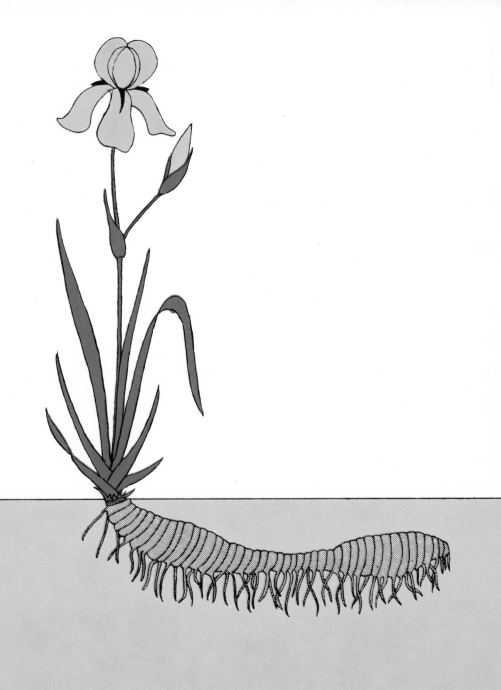

Only green plants in sunlight can make food from the air

and from the earth.

No matter how hard the sun shines, animals can not make food from the air and from the earth.

Animals must get their food by eating plants or by eating animals that eat food made by plants.

So all the animals above ground

depend on plants for food

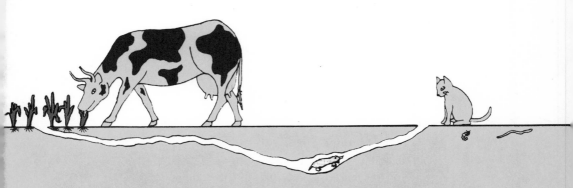

and so do all the animals below ground.